What Makes Plants Grow?

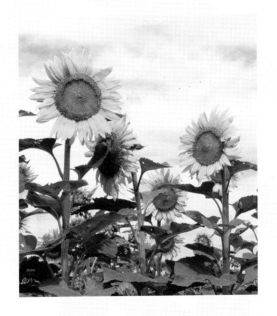

Karen Clevidence

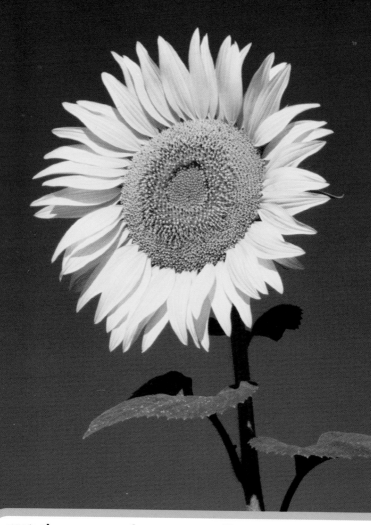

What makes sunflowers grow?

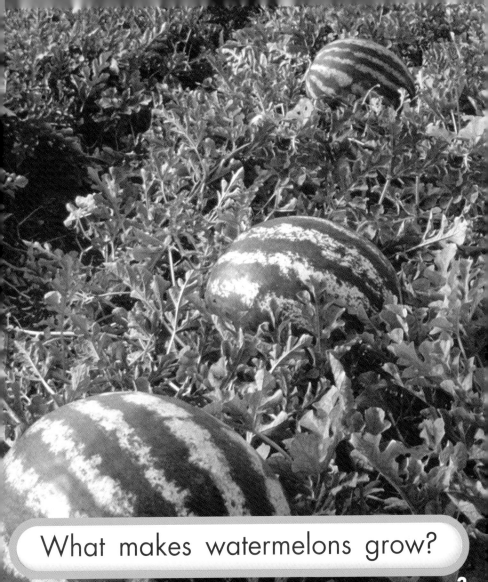

What makes watermelons grow?

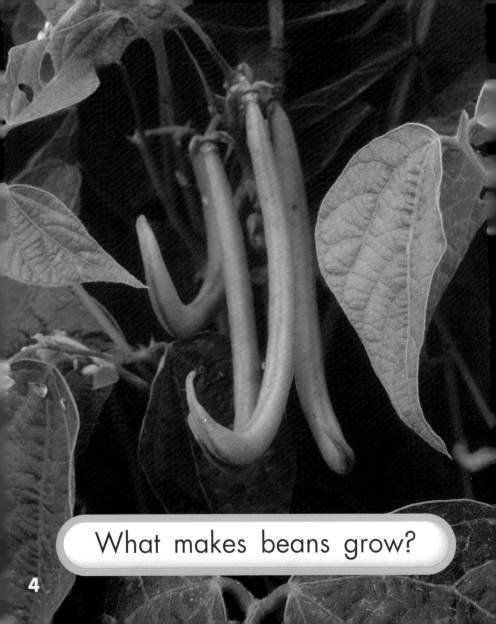

What makes beans grow?

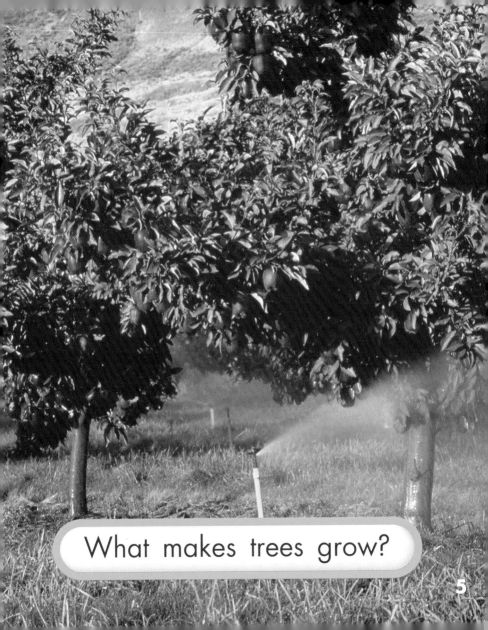

What makes trees grow?

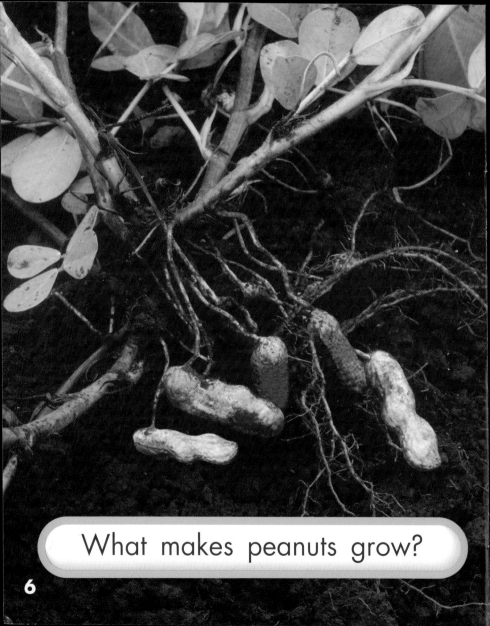

What makes peanuts grow?

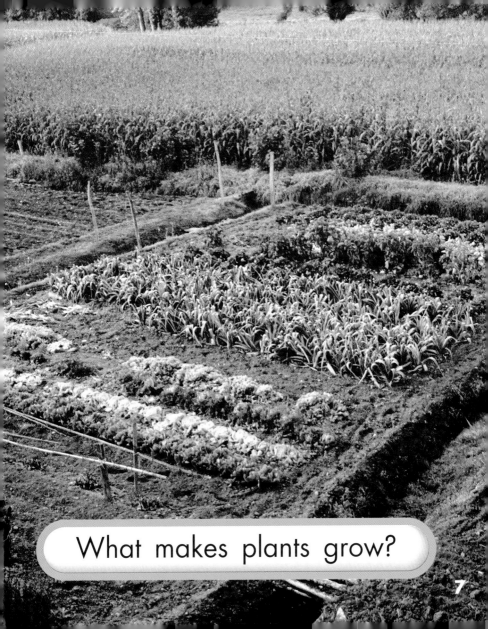

What makes plants grow?

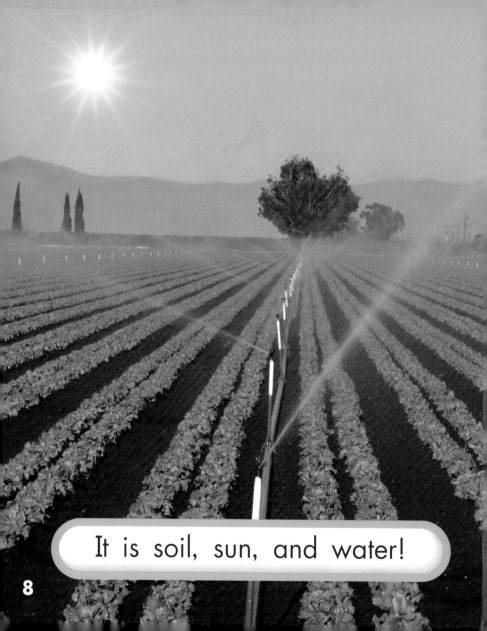

It is soil, sun, and water!